Qi-Gong and Kuji-In

A Practical Guide to
An Oriental Esoteric Experience

by MahaVajra

F.Lepine Publishing

www.kujiin.com

© François Lépine, 2016

ISBN: 978-1-926659-25-1

My gratitude to the Masters that have
taught me this Sacred knowledge.

May you have a blessed experience
as you practice the powerful techniques found in this book.

- Maha Vajra

Table of Contents

Introduction

The human body, despite the fact that we use it every day of our lives from birth to death, is still the center of many profound mysteries. The mysteries of the heart and mind (which seem to defy the ability of science to dissect and understand) are even greater. By comparison, the mysteries of the Spirit are beyond the reaches of our imagination. For this reason, we begin our spiritual work with the study and practices that use the human body as a tool. Through our personal research, we will find many spiritual secrets are hidden in the workings of our physical and tangible experience.

We could write an entire book for each chapter we have written here. However, we wish to concentrate on the practical aspects of each of the techniques we will be showing you. Thus, we will summarize a great deal of information in but a few lines. There are also a few technical words that you may want to understand before you start learning about this mystical art. These words are essential to your understanding of the rest of the book, and we will repeat their names often to make their assimilation easier. These new terms are in bold below, followed by an explanation of their meaning and use.

Meridians: There are many circuits of energy in the human body. Most of them start or end at an extremity such as the fingers or toes. The Chinese refer to these energy circuits as Meridians. Both Qi-Gong and Kuji-In employ certain tools to stimulate and direct the energy emanating from these energy circuits in order to heal your body on the energetic and physical levels and to help you manifest your desires. The techniques you will use to work with energy include: breathing exercises, visualizations (called mandalas), chants/prayers (called mantras) and hand positions (called mudras). Qi-Gong and Kuji-In use these mandalas, mantras and mudras, along with specific exercises, to help you connect with your Higher Self. This book also provides the conceptual context that will make it possible for you to successfully use these techniques.

Mudra: A "mudra" is a hand gesture or a hand position that is employed to bring into effect the flow of energies that terminate or start at the fingertips.

Mantra: The energy of the body can also be stimulated through sound. A "mantra" is a sound, which can take the form of either a short word or a more complex prayer. A mantra will stimulate specific energy patterns within and around you.

Mandala: Above all, the symbols and imageries in your mind affect the flow and the manifestations of the energies you use. A "mandala" is a symbol or image that is visualized in order to engage the mind in active participation with an energy work or a spiritual process.

Mudra, mantra and mandala: these are three simple tools that can enhance your entire spiritual experience. These tools affect the energies in your physical and spiritual body. When combined, they can greatly enhance your personal development. They can produce any kind of effect, from accelerating the healing of the body to aiding you in developing psychic abilities. These tools are a part of a sacred knowledge called Qi-Gong, which means "working with energy" or "energy practice".

The main topic of this book series is the art called "Kuji-In" that redefines your vision of the world around you. Practicing its techniques will slowly reveal to you a vision of the universe that you could not have anticipated before you began, because it allows your limited human mind to expand its vision, to perceive the Source of All. This spiritual method will surely help you progress on your path to the realization of your full potential. Here follows a Buddhist contemplation that I hope will inspire you about the state of mind that the Kuji-In intends to develop in each practitioner.

The Buddha said: "I consider the positions of Kings and Rulers as that of dust motes. I observe treasures of gold and gems as so many bricks and pebbles. I look upon the finest silken robes as tattered rags. I see myriad worlds of the universe as small seeds of fruit, and the greatest lake in India as a drop of oil on my foot. I perceive the teachings of the world to be the illusion of magicians. I discern the highest conception of emancipation as a golden brocade in a dream, and I view the holy path of the illuminated ones as flowers appearing in one's eyes. I see meditation as a pillar of a mountain, Nirvana as a nightmare of daytime. I look upon the judgment of right and wrong as the serpentine Dance of a dragon, and the rise and fall of beliefs as but traces left by the four seasons."

Above all, let the knowledge of this book be assimilated through experience rather than isolated intellectual analysis. Take the time to contemplate the feeling each technique evokes for you. Pay attention to your body, your heart and your mind. Eventually, you will become aware of your Spirit. All of the technical words will be surrounded by practical instructions, and this will help your mind make the necessary links. Trust yourself and have a good learning experience.

Summarized Theory

The Buddhist, Taoist and Hindu teachings contain the fundamental wisdom that can be found behind most Oriental practices. All the teachings of the mantra's sounds, the mudras gestures and the mandala's symbols come from these sources, as well as from the many applications of meditation those teachings utilize. Chinese medicine is also a very important source of knowledge for Qi-Gong practitioners.

The martial arts that were developed by the Shao-Lin monks use a mystical secret science to control the energy in the body. This profound science is called Qi-Gong. Qi is energy in its manifested form, and Gong is the practical method of application. Therefore, Qi-Gong methods are the means or techniques of controlling the flow of energy inside your body. After a while, with a lot of practice, you can also experiment with the manifestation of Qi outside your body.

The most popular form of Qi-Gong in North America and Europe is Tai Qi Chuan. The art of Qi-Gong existed long before the martial artists incorporated it in their fighting styles. Therefore, there are a lot of Qi-Gong practices that are very easy on the body. These practices are not linked with any specific fighting techniques, and it is not necessary to learn to fight to learn these techniques.

Like many esoteric philosophies, the Buddhists teach that, in order to attain spiritual illumination, one must undertake the necessary exercises with a sincere heart. The secrets of healing, the ability to see beyond ordinary reality, the gift of communication from mind to mind, these are all aspects of the Buddhist's magical system. Like every group of Alchemists, they also seek to expand their lifespan beyond the normal period. Yet none of these abilities will manifest for you unless you begin with the proper attitude.

The Qi-Gong techniques shown in the first lessons are the basic methods which will enhance your ability to experience spiritual energies. After you have achieved the ability to sense energy, we will concentrate on the practical aspects of the oriental esoteric science of Kuji-In. We encourage you to learn more about Chinese Medicine and the channels of energy in the body. It is also very important for you to choose a meditation technique and to meditate frequently if you want to benefit from the enormous potential of the methods explained in this manual. For beginners, a simple meditation technique is provided in this book. As you learn more and as you diligently practice what you have learned, your experiences with Qi-Gong and Kuji-In will improve.

Oriental Energy Systems: Jin, Qi, Shen

In the last section we explained that energy takes shape in a broad range of manifestations: light, movement, electricity, life... Thus we find that energy will manifest in your body in many ways. We have classified them here as three types of energy: Jin, Qi and Shen. These are the energies that flow in the physical body according to Traditional Chinese Medicine. They take other names in occidental occult philosophy, and we will speak about these other terminologies elsewhere.

Jin

The energy that directly influences the physical plane is called Jin. It is the power that is converted into physical movement; it is heat energy, and it is the force behind every action. Jin can be converted from Qi, which is a more subtle energy. Many methods for converting Qi into Jin involve compressing Qi until it is dense enough to become available on the physical plane, where it can manifest. Jin can produce heat, it can create more intense electric currents in our nervous system, it can heal our body more quickly than Qi alone and it can augment physical strength. Jin is energy acting on gross matter. It usually flows through the lower abdomen.

You will develop the Jin level of energy through the use of breathing exercises and Qi-Gong practices. Jin will be used in many of the physical practices you will be learning in the next several sections. Jin assists us in developing willpower and self-confidence. Willpower and self-confidence help the Jin to manifest physically.

Qi

Qi is energy in its ethereal form. It is our life force. It is bioelectricity. It is naturally used by the body for all of our life functions and it is used by the brain to operate. Qi can move from one place to another before it is converted to the active form of Jin or to the elevated form of energy known as Shen. We wish to develop and accumulate Qi because it is easy to use and because it offers us the widest range of applications. Breathing techniques enhance the movement of Qi in the body, as well as our ability to make effective use of mental imagery.

The more freely Qi can move in and around your body, the healthier you will be, and the more clearly you will be able to think.

Qi can be stored inside the body battery for later use (more on this in other chapters). Qi can move through the body and, with experience, outside the body. It can be transferred to someone else for healing purposes, or for the exchange of Qi to another person. Great Chinese doctors use it in all sorts of medical techniques. Martial artists use it to augment their power and speed. It is also spelled Chi in the case of Chi -Gong, or Ki. The Chinese and Japanese characters are not alphabetical; they are pictograms, so their spelling in English varies.

Shen

Shen is the spiritual aspect of energy. It is more volatile and harder to feel. It is always present, but the average person won't even know it is there. It is the energy used in internal spiritual methods like prayer and meditation. As we develop Shen, we also develop our Spirit and elevate our consciousness. Little information about Shen is available to the average person. In fact, a practitioner only becomes aware of its existence after extended training.

Chakras

We will be very brief regarding the definition of the "Chakras". The topic of Chakras is a subject too vast to cover in detail in this book, but we will give you the basic information needed to use the different techniques shown here.

The Chakras are the main energy centers found in the physical body. Each Chakra has specific primary functions you will need to know. These will be described along with the techniques that activate those functions. There are seven major Chakras.

1- Base Chakra: Located at the base of the spine; extends from the base of the pelvis at the front of your body, to the coccyx at the back of your body. The base Chakra thus covers the entire base of your body.

2- Navel Chakra: Located about one inch below your navel.

3- Solar Plexus Chakra: Located at the solar plexus, right under your sternum.

4- Heart Chakra: Located directly in the middle of the sternum, in front of your heart.

5- Throat Chakra: Located in the little indentation of bones at the base of your throat.

6- Third Eye Chakra: Located between your eyebrows.

7- Crown Chakra: found at the top of your head, with the center point exactly on top of your head, but spreading down to surround part of your head, around the forehead and the back of the skull.

Another important Chakra is called the "Jade Gate", and it is found at the back of the head, on the pointy bone at the back of the skull.

Behind the Navel Chakra, in the middle of the body, inside the lower abdomen, is a place which is called the "Dan-tian" in Chinese Medicine; we will refer to it in our practices. It is in the Dan-tian where the energy of the body is gathered and stored for later use.

It is not necessary to remember all these Chakras right now. We will give you the information you need about the Chakras throughout the book.

Techniques

As you start training, we encourage you to eat well and exercises regularly to keep your body in good health. Some of the techniques you will be learning are more demanding than others. Respect your limits, while always trying to go beyond them safely. Since some of these techniques might raise your body temperature aggressively, we encourage you to drink a lot of water.

It is good to experiment with all of the techniques at least once, until you discover which ones you prefer. Once you decide what works best for you, feel free to spend more time on the practices you prefer. Follow you heart and do not doubt yourself. You should use at least one physical practice, one heart practice, one practice for the mind and one for the Spirit. The first subtle results will come quickly, then a longer period of time might pass before you see any tangible results. During this plateau period, your body will be accumulating and increasing your energy level. Do not begin your training by focusing on the end-results you may eventually attain; instead, enjoy the immediate benefits that these exercises provide. Before all else, seek Love. The power associated with these practices will come by itself. If you seek power, it will take much more time for the effects to manifest, and they will not be as impressive.

The Physical Body

Breathing

Normal and Reversed Breathing

Normal Breathing:

Normal Breathing is very different from the automatic breathing cycle that keeps you alive when you are not thinking about breathing. The reason is simple: no one really breathes correctly without thinking about it. Most people take in only 11 ml of oxygen per minute, far below the minimum oxygen your body needs to be healthy. A Normal Breath is a healthy breath.

An inhalation should fill your lungs almost completely without straining your abdomen or diaphragm. The breath should naturally fill your abdomen, without raising your upper torso. A deep breath should not even make your upper ribs move. Place your hand over your heart, where your ribs connect to your sternum, between your solar plexus and your throat. Take a deep breath and feel to see if your ribs are moving. If they do, you are filling your upper lungs too much, and not enough air is getting to the bottom of your lungs. Although it is impossible to keep your rib cage totally immobile (which is not the objective) it should move as little as possible without requiring too much effort.

When you exhale, let your abdomen rest until the air doesn't come out naturally anymore, and then pull your abdomen in slightly without force. It won't completely empty your lungs. If your ribs are moving inward or downward too much, it means you had to lift them upward when you inhaled, or that you filled the upper part of your lungs too much.

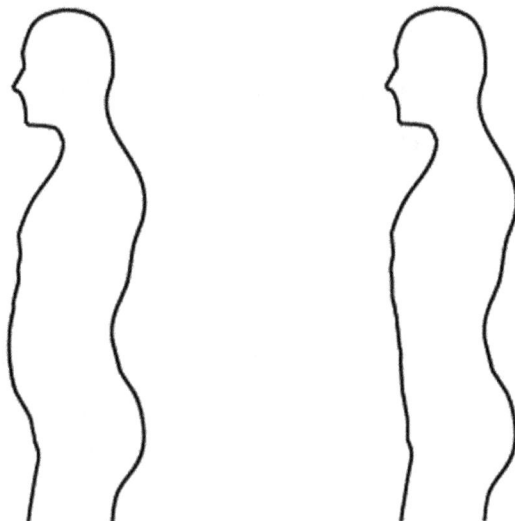

Breath in
Abdomen out
Upper chest normal

Breath out
Abdomen normal
Upper chest normal

When you breathe normally, it is your abdomen that pushes out slightly and pulls in slightly, (as you inhale and exhale). The breathing cycle should not require excessive force, but it should fill your lungs up to 80% of your maximum capacity. To fill your lungs to 100% of their capacity requires effort, and it is not natural. Breathing out with force and pulling in your abdomen slightly at the end of the breath empties your lungs to 10% or 20% of their capacity. Just as it is not healthy to fill your lungs to 100%, it is not healthy to empty them completely; to empty your lungs totally requires the application of more force than to bring them to a natural state.

To learn this for yourself, try filling your lungs completely (without hurting yourself), while keeping your rib cage as immobile as possible. Then, hold the air in for 10 seconds and breathe out completely, holding your breath out for 10 seconds. Let all your muscles relax and allow your body to breathe without influencing it, while you think about the difference between these two ways of breathing. Now, take in a Normal Breath, filling your lungs down to your abdomen with only a slight effort. Hold the air in for 3 seconds, and then let it out without any other effort than a slight pulling inward of your abdomen at the end of exhalation.

This is what is meant by a "Normal Breath". Normal Breathing will be used in all of the techniques that focus on the elevation of self, such as meditation, mental and spiritual training. The Reversed Breath is used in physical development, to open the channels of energy in your body and to enhance your ability to manifest your Qi on the physical plane.

Reversed Breathing

To clearly understand the principles of Reversed Breathing, you must first practice accurate Normal Breathing. It is important to keep your rib cage almost motionless while doing the Reversed Breathing. You should also understand the principles of Jin, Qi and Shen in order for this practice to be effective.

The Reversed Breathing cycle is used to concentrate or compress your Qi in a way that will make it denser, compressing it, so it can become available on the physical plane. It is used to produce Jin from your Qi. When you compact the Qi, you will feel heat. This is the Jin.

To clarify this for you, forget about the Normal Breathing method for a moment and let yourself breathe instinctively. Imagine yourself in a situation where you are very alert, perhaps needing to defend yourself, thus requiring that you are ready for immediate action. While closing your fists, take in a quick, deep breath without thinking. Most people will notice that the abdomen automatically pulls in when you are breathing in, and it pushes out slightly when you exhale. Experiment a bit with this breathing.

Breath in
Abdomen pulled in
Upper chest normal

Breath out
Abdomen let out
Upper chest normal

When in Danger, the body automatically does a Reversed Breath, getting ready to pour energy into physical action. The quick breath mentioned above was only meant as an example. For the Reversed Breath method, the breath should be drawn in as smoothly as the Normal Breath unless stated otherwise.

When we are working with methods that focus on manifesting physical phenomena, we will be experiment it with Reversed Breathing. The upper rib cage still doesn't move, and you should still breathe slowly and comfortably. As you breathe in, contract your abdomen, pulling it in slightly. As you breathe out, release your abdominal muscles completely, pushing out slightly at the end of the exhalation, without force.

Radial Qi Gathering method

Before you do anything that utilizes Qi, you must have Qi reserves to work with. Working without reserves of Qi will deplete your own life force, which should be avoided at all cost. Gathering Qi is quite simple, and you can do it just about anywhere and anytime as long as you aren't doing something that requires concentration. For example, don't do this when you're in a moving car. When you gather Qi, you and everyone around you will get a little bit more prone to lose their concentration. For example, everyone could get sleepy, or hyper, or feel strange sensations in their body, especially if they are not used to feeling Qi. Moreover, you will need to be able to use your concentration for the visualizations that are necessary to successfully gather, store, and move Qi. The energy that you envision is real and it will follow your concentration. As you visualize it traveling with your breath down to the area below your navel, the Qi will be moved to your Dan-tian. When you visualize compressing it in your Dan-tian, this too will actually occur. You may use the pictures as a guide, and you will find it useful to think of the energy you are moving as a white cloud which flows like a stream wherever you direct it with your mind.

Place you palms on your Dan-tian, which is just below your navel (fig. 1). Men should have their left palm inside, touching their Dan-tian, with their right palm over their left. Women should have their right palm inside, with their left palm over their right. If you are standing, bend your knees slightly. If you are sitting, try to keep your spine straight, and do not cross your legs.

As you inhale, visualize white light coming from all around you, penetrating all the pores of your skin, flowing into

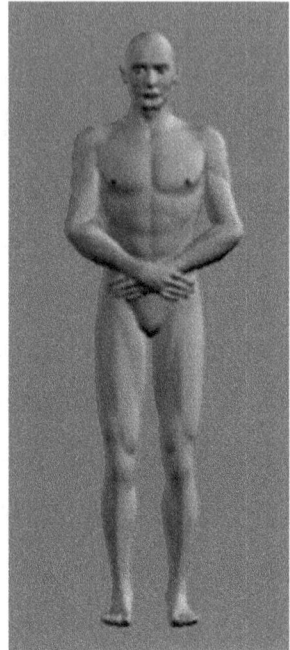

Fig. 1

your body and filling your inner Dan-tian. Remember that what you visualize is actually occurring. As you exhale, all of this white energy is condensed into a concentrated ball of light in your inner Dan-tian, in the middle of your body just below the level of your navel. Gather Qi by breathing normally, deeply, and calmly. Take in Qi from all around you and concentrate it in your inner Dan-tian.

Active Gathering

Stand up, take a few Normal Breaths and relax. Slightly bend your knees and begin.

As you breathe in, imagine a white light coming from above you, which enters through the top of your head rather like a white wind, descending in a continuous flow to your Dan-tian. Please

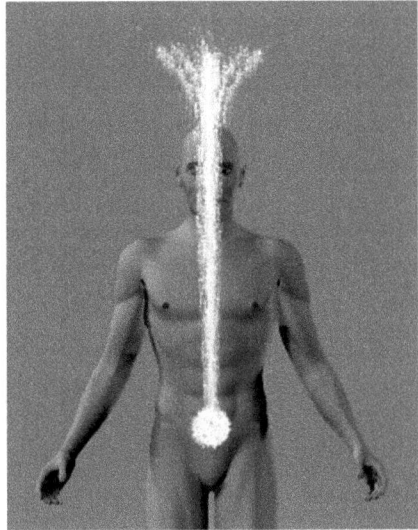

Fig. 2

refer to fig. 2 below. You may use this figure as guide for your visualizations. As you breathe out, the energy remains in your lower abdomen and becomes a ball of light. Take nine relaxed breaths, absorbing Qi (the white light) from the area above your head. You may find that you tighten the muscles of your abdomen and arms when you try this for the first time. That is a normal reflex. Practice using just your will to draw the energy down, while keeping your muscles relaxed.

In the next exercise, you will draw energy into both hands, through the trunk of your body, and down into the Dan tian. You will inhale, and draw energy in through both hands simultaneously. To do this, extend your arms out to your sides, with your palms facing away from you; absorb the energy through the middle of your palms, drawing the energy through your arms, the trunk of your body, and down into your Dan-tian. Repeat this sequence, (inhale and draw the energy down to the Dan-tian) nine times. Relax your body and make this entire process as effortless as possible.

Next you will repeat this process with both of your feet, drawing the wind-like energy up into the soles of your feet, and up through your legs, directing the flow to your Dan-tian. When you have the energy centered in your Dan-tian, visualize the white energy ball growing stronger and stronger with each of the nine breaths.

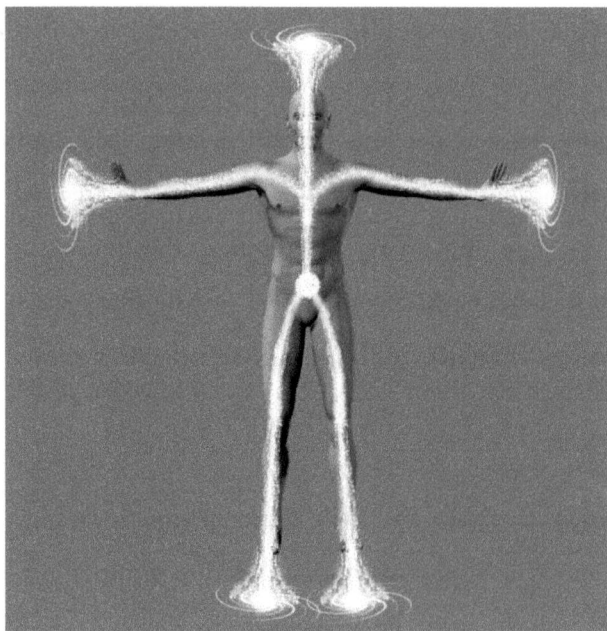

Fig. 3

Once you've taken nine breaths, while drawing the energy into your Dan-tian through each of the 5 centers, (filling your abdomen from the area above your head, and from both of your hands and feet), you will proceed to draw energy through all 5 centers at the same time, using all five entry points simultaneously, and filling your Dan-tian with nine breaths of energy. (fig. 3)

Finish this exercise by placing your palms over your Dan-tian and taking a few Normal Breaths. This will help to store the energy you have gathered.

Feeling the Flow of Qi

While your body is taking in oxygen and circulating it, it is also naturally circulating bioelectric energy. This energy is used to manage bodily functions and to sustain life. The calmer and more smoothly this energy flows, the healthier we are and the more clearly we think. Our emotions are influenced by this bioelectric energy flow as well as by our hormones.

In the same way that we have learned to draw energy into the Dan-tian by concentrating on our breathing and visualizing the bioelectric energy as it follows our breath into our Solar Plexus, we can also concentrate on our breathing and direct the bioelectricity in other ways. For example, we can make this energy flow through our body simply by desiring it to do so.

When we wish to lift an arm, we don't need to know how the blood flows in the veins and how the neural energy stimulates the ADP of the muscle fibers to make them contract... all we need to do is "will it" and the arm lifts. A baby can lift its arm as well as a scientist. It only has to desire to do so.

In order to cause this to occur according to your desires, you simply need to imagine where the energy is and where you want it to go, and the Qi will behave accordingly, following the motion of your mental image. With time and practice, you will be able to feel this movement of Qi as if it was a wind flowing through your body. Some people describe this as a feeling that water is flowing from the source of the Qi to wherever they direct it. The traditional name for the art of causing this energy to flow in accordance with your desires is Qi-Gong, meaning "the practice of Qi."

Breathing will enhance the movement of Qi. Visualization alone will also cause Qi to flow, but not enough to make your practice truly efficient. In order for this practice to be truly effective, you must breathe properly, mentally visualizing the flow, then you must desire that the bioelectric energy move to the specified location. This is similar to wanting to move your arm; you desire it and it occurs, even though the rest of your body remains motionless. It is an isolated action, affecting only that part of you that you desire to move. Breathing normally is essential to the development of your energy channels and to the use of Qi in its many applications. When you breathe in, you are drawing energy into you, and when you breathe out, that energy will flow to wherever you direct it. Clear visualizations, proper breathing and the proper use of desire are crucial to effective movement of the Qi.

It is important that you follow the basic training process outlined here so you can correctly train your mind to visualize the good energy moving according to your desires. We strongly recommend that you never imagine any chaotic or disordered energy moving through your body, because it might disturb your regular bodily functions.

A step by step approach is necessary to develop your mental ability to control Qi in your body. As you acquire the necessary knowledge and experience in the art of directing this energy flow, you will be able to feel the effect of your training and understand the different applications of Qi-Gong more quickly and more completely.

Technique for Learning to Sense Qi:

Once you've practiced the Gathering Qi method, your body has a little more Qi than it normally does, and this makes it easier for you to feel the Qi. Never do any Qi exercises without filling yourself up with Qi beforehand, otherwise you could use up your basic life-force or Bioelectric reserves and this can lead to undesirable side-effects, such as fatigue or illness.

Take a few natural breaths. Put your right palm over your left arm without touching it, maintaining at least a distance of one inch. You will now use the Reversed Breathing technique. As you breathe in and contract your abdomen a bit, fill your right hand with Qi by imagining that your hand is filled with white light/wind. As you breathe out, let your abdomen relax, visualize the Qi emanating from your right hand to the surface of your left arm. Use your will/desire as well as your imagination to achieve this effect. Move your right hand over the skin surface as you begin to notice a light sensation emanating directly from your right hand.

Qi can trigger sensations of heat, cold, a windy sensation, a tickling, or nothing at all when you are first trying this. After taking a few breaths, and using your palm to emanate the Qi, try to emanate Qi by pointing with your fingers. To do this, keep your right arm straight and point the fingers of your left hand at your right arm, moving your left hand over the fingers of your right arm and up to the elbow, then very slowly back and forth while you continue Reversed Breathing and the visualization. Eventually, you will feel the Qi flowing.

Qi-Gong

Small and Grand Circulation

The following is a limited summary of the Small and Grand Circulation. There is an enormous amount of knowledge available on this subject, and we recommend that you learn more about it after you learn these basic practices.

There are two main passageways of Qi, one of which run down the middle of the front of your body and the other up the middle of your back. The channel in front is called the "Conception Vessel", and the one in the back, along the spine, is called the "Governing Vessel".

Small Circulation

We will use the Reversed Breath for this technique, as you visualize white light flowing through your vessels. Figure 4 will help you understand the trajectory for this visualization. Using the reverse breathing, you will inhale once while you perform steps #1 to #4, and then exhale at step 5.

Take a few Normal Breaths and relax.

Begin your inhalation, and visualize white Qi emanating from your inner Dan-tian. As you contract your abdomen, visualize the Qi moving down into your Conception Vessel (#1). The Qi keeps flowing gently down and under your groin as you contract your sexual organs and your perineum (#2). The Qi flows back into the coccyx and up as you contract the cheeks of your buttocks. (#3) Next you complete the inhalation as the Qi moves into your spine at the level of your inner Dan-tian (#4). As you breathe out, letting go of your abdomen, the Qi moves back in your inner Dan-tian (#5).

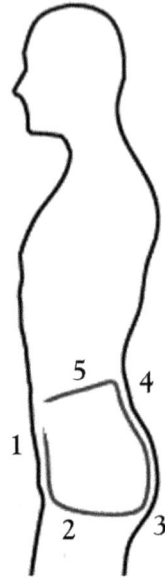

Fig. 4

Start with a few consecutive small circulations and try to feel the Qi flowing. It is recommended that you do nine complete loops at a time, and then relax. Perform these exercises slowly and comfortably.

Grand Circulation

Fig. 5

Using figure 5 as your visualization guide, complete one inhalation while you perform steps #1 to #5. Exhale naturally, without visualization.

Take a few Normal Breaths and relax.

As you begin your inhalation, contract your abdomen, and visualize white Qi emanating from your inner Dan-tian and moving down into your Conception Vessel at (#1). The Qi keeps flowing gently down and under your body as you contract your sexual organs and your perineum (#2). The Qi flows back into the coccyx and up your back, as you contract the cheeks of your buttocks (#3). Keeping your abdomen, perineum, and buttocks contracted, visualize the Qi flowing up your back to the top of your head at (#4). Finish your inhalation as the Qi starts moving back down your forehead and nose (#5). As you breathe out, let go of all contractions, and the Qi will naturally move back down the front of your body, through the Conception Vessel, and down to the point at #1 again.

Perform nine circulations at a time, then relax. Always do these exercises slowly and comfortably.

Dance of the Dragon

The Qi-Gong Dragon Dance has many positive benefits, from healing your body, to elevating your energy level. It is a bodily prayer calling for your Divine Spirit to flow through your body. It will activate circulation, develop balance, stimulate the endocrine system, improve your biological defensive mechanisms, provoke regeneration, and much more.

As a pleasing side effect, it will help your body convert fat into useful energy. It also elevates your body temperature a bit, further contributing to weight loss. By twisting your hips and moving your thighs, you will also reshape your body and develop flexibility.

You might have to read the following paragraphs a few times to understand the next technique well enough to do it. You will move your joined hands in a "three circle trajectory" (figure 6), while balancing your hips in the opposite direction. This will place your spine in a balancing S shape (figure 7). Follow numbers #1 through #8 along the path and memorize those steps. The circles cross at your throat, Solar Plexus and perineum, then Solar Plexus again and throat again, to complete a figure the looks like a three-loop eight.

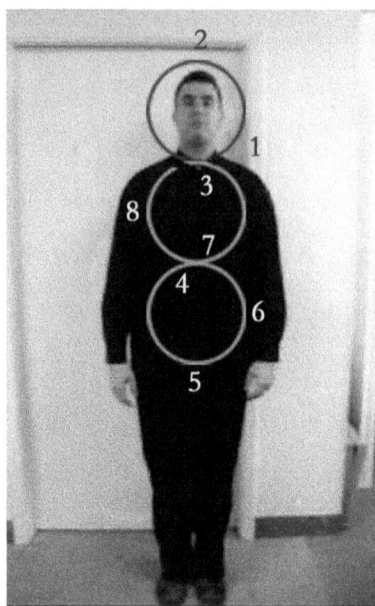

Fig. 6

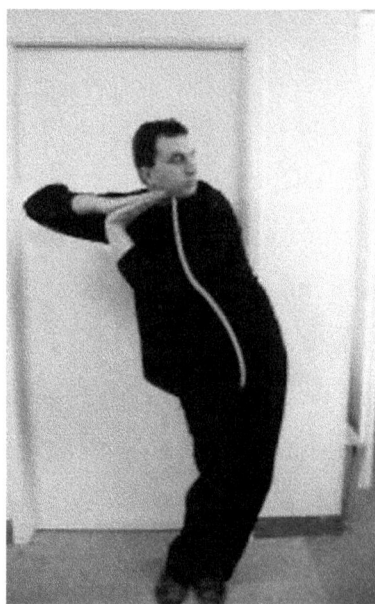

Fig. 7

When your hands are in the middle of your body, your hips are also in the middle, and you look downward a bit. When your hands are to your right, your hips are to your left, and you are looking left. When your hands are to your left, your hips are to your right and you are looking right. As you crouch down, you will also bend your legs until you are half crouched, with your hands at number 5 on figure 6's path. The top circle of the path will be completed more in front of you than above your head.

The Dance is performed in two steps. The first step is the active movement of the Dragon, and the second step is a contemplative series of breaths, without movements. We provide photos below to help you understand and execute the Dance. Go slowly at first, getting used to every movement before you do the entire Dance in a single fluid motion.

Do the entire Dance of the Dragon once, and breathe normally for 30 seconds, keeping your hands in front on your Dan-tian. Focus on happiness and youth. Keep your spine straight and smile a bit, even if you have to force a fake smile. The Dance of the Dragon takes about one minute per repetition. Perform the repetitions in multiples of three. Doing nine repetitions in the morning, nine at noon and nine in the evening, will create great changes in your physical body and your energy vessels.

Step 1
Be at peace. Visualize
yourself as young and happy.

Step 2
Palms together, in front
of your perineum.

Step 3
Hands up to your chin.

Step 4
Hands towards your left, hips a
little towards your right.

Step 5
Hands in front, hips behind,
lower your head between
your arms.

Step 6
Hands to your right, hips a
little to your left.

Step 7
Hands to your right,
pointing left, hips far to your left.
Start crouching.

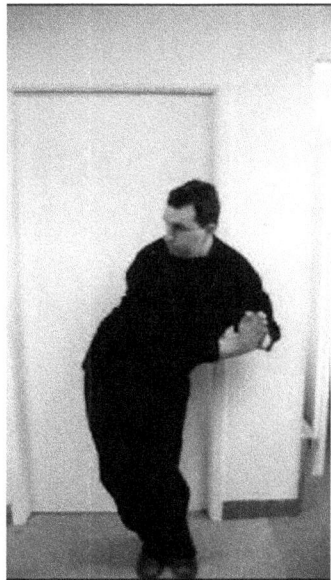

Step 8
Hands pass your throat, then to
your left; hips move to your right,
spine in S shape.

Step 9
Hands pass your Solar Plexus,
right hand inside,
as you crouch lower..

Step 10
Hands move to your lower right,
hips and knees move to your left,
crouching more.

Step 11
Hands flat at your perineum, left
hand inside, right hand outside.

Step 12
Hands move to your left,
un-crouch a bit.

Step 13
Hands pass your solar plexus,
and move to your right,
hips move to your left.

Step 14
Hands pass your throat and move
to your left, hips move to your
right as you straighten up.

Step 15
Hands move up above your
head and a bit to the front.
Stand straight.

Stand 16
Stand on the tips of your toes
by lifting your heels from the
floor, bend a bit forward, stay
balanced a few seconds

Step 17
With your feet back on the
ground, form a triangle with your
index fingers and thumbs, as you
lower your hands.

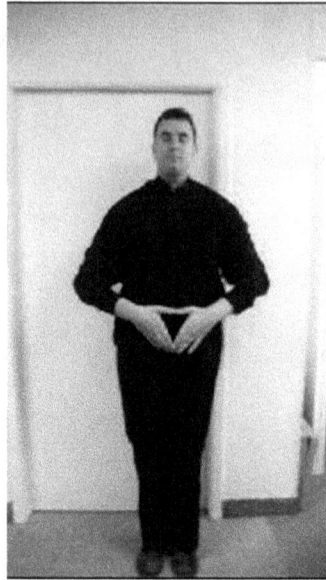

Step 18
Hold your hands in the triangle
in front of your Dan-tian.
Breathe normally for
30 seconds.

Once you become used to the movements, combine the breathing with the Dragon form. In all the movements where you raise your hands, inhale. As you lower your hands, exhale. The effects of the Dance will be greatly enhanced.

The Elixir of Life

The theory and practice of the techniques of Life Extension are quite simple, but it takes a long time to achieve the desired results. Then again, you have the rest of your life to reach your goals, so you can enjoy practicing the techniques as you extend your lifespan.

I recommend you learn more about lifespan extension, via the various videos I made freely available on my Youtube channel. Three are many philosophical concepts to realize before you can greatly expand your lifespan. For now, we include a simple technique to practice daily.

Breathe in Life in the form of white light, through the middle of your palms, the middle of the base of your feet, and the top of your head. Each time you inhale, breathe in Qi through your 5 extremities, directing it towards your abdomen and concentrating it in your inner Dan-tian. Each time you breathe out, air is exhaled while all energy remains inside your body, but you should not really concentrate on this aspect for this technique. Let your exhalation remain natural and relaxed.

Once you are able to visualize the Qi becoming concentrated into a powerful ball (6 inches wide) inside your abdomen, relax, and visualize the ball becoming increasingly dense. Imagine that it is increasingly tangible, real. It will be converted into an intense red pill of bioelectric energy that you can even feel physically, so concentrated has it become. Continue to build up the red pill of life in your visualization. As your bodily fluids pass through your abdomen, the red pill of Life will slowly release its serum into your bloodstream, which will circulate through your entire body, filling it with the clear red light of Life. Visualize the red pill of Life Energy continuing to become a concentrated center of living red energy in your inner Dan-tian.

This practice is only a part of what can be done to extend your lifespan. The practice of praying, thanking God if it's part of your belief system, chanting mantras, or engaging in whatever practices you believe in to show gratitude and connection to your Creator, will benefit you as well. These practices will raise your energy level and permit good circulation of energy in your body. To extend your lifespan, you must also expand your consciousness. Meditations in which you empty your mind of everything are highly recommended.

Of the Heart

The Mantra of Compassion

Before you learn about the doorways of power, you need to develop the attitude required to access and use any type of spiritual power. The way you see and define your life will also determine the specific way the powerful energy of your Spirit will manifest through you. Having a negative perception of life will definitely have equally negative consequences for the way the essence of the spiritual energies will manifest through you. With proper training, you can manifest only the joyful and happy events you desire in your life.

We recommend that you begin your inner spiritual development by focusing on developing compassion, which is one of the most powerful sources of energy for the manifestation of the Buddha in your body and in your daily life.

Om Mani Padme Hum

The mantra (prayer), Om Mani Padme Hum, said out loud or silently to oneself, invokes the powerful, benevolent attention and blessings of Chenrezig, the Buddhist embodiment of compassion. It is said that viewing the written form of the mantra has potent effects, acting as a talisman.

ཨོཾ་མ་ཎི་པདྨེ་ཧཱུྃ།

It is also said that all the teachings of the Buddha are contained in this mantra: Om Mani Padme Hum, and that it cannot really be translated into a simple phrase or sentence.

Chant it as often as you wish, and you will develop compassion and attract compassion.

Implication

The concept of evolving quickly and easily is a common topic in this "New Age". Many people wish to develop tremendous power while taking little responsibility for the consequences of their use of that power. They want to invest very little time and energy, while reaping huge rewards. It is possible for you to evolve very quickly, but it is also necessary that you develop personal responsibility before you achieve these gains. This cannot be avoided.

Value and a Fair Exchange

It is important to demonstrate your appreciation of the value in the sacred knowledge that you will acquire here. You must learn how to cherish this knowledge and understand that you must not give it freely to someone who might then destroy or mutilate it. This occult knowledge is too important to be treated as anything other than your most precious possession. You must keep it for yourself, and reveal it only when the seeker before you has shown signs of understanding and respect. There is a spiritual cost to revealing occult secrets of great value to someone before they have shown the mandatory respect. When a monk wanted to learn something from his Master, he had to work hard all day, and bring some food with him (to give the Master). Then, the Master would see that there was a balance in the exchange, and he would reveal some esoteric knowledge to the seeker. There must not be any abuse in this exchange. The exchange must be fair and balanced. You must never destroy your life to acquire occult knowledge, but you surely will not acquire any knowledge of great value without some kind of effort and sacrifice.

You will develop great power only when you feel within yourself that you value and cherish this sacred knowledge, and when you behave in ways that will protect this knowledge. We call this attitude the "Sense of the Sacred". This "Sense of the Sacred" is a required prerequisite to the achievement of the greatest power in any occult system.

Time and Willpower

You will not develop any psychic powers by trying a method once for five minutes. You will not even attain anything by trying some technique for an hour, and then immediately quitting because of a lack of results.

To develop great power, you must practice a minimum of five minutes per day, every day of the week. Once a week, you must practice for at least one full hour. Do something everyday, even a simple salutation to your altar, but do it.

To evolve more quickly, you may practice the exercises twenty minutes each day. All of those who have acted with determination to make progress on their own spiritual path have achieved some transformation and elevation from within, with this kind of consistent effort. If nothing happens inside, you might not be infusing yourself with a "Sacred" attitude, with respect for the value of the knowledge you desire. Nonetheless, you should give yourself time for the results to manifest in you.

Some very uncompromising students, who are very committed to getting results, have used these techniques for thirty minutes every day. After only a few months, these devoted students are feeling intense flows of energy, getting results in their personal life, and becoming aware of patterns in their behavior they had never noticed before. In addition to these practices, the most uncompromising students studied esoteric knowledge, kept a sacred attitude, and took care of their bodies.

Gather your resolve, build your determination, and then do it. If you practice only five minutes per day, every day, you will get results.

Karma and Dharma

We will not write an extensive essay about Karma and Dharma here, since a lot of documentation is available on these subjects elsewhere; Instead of a long diatribe, we will summarize the main concepts and give you a daily exercise to practice for your own personal growth.

Karma is the result or consequence of your past deeds. You get from life what you put into it; you reap from the field in the fall what you sowed as seed in the spring; you receive an eye for an eye. Every action you take will result in a reaction in the Universe, and that reaction will eventually rebound back to you (as Karmic justice). To perceive your life on a spiritual level, you must begin to understand that any action you take, even those you took in a past life, will reproduce itself in your life today in the form of a lesson that may include a bit of suffering. These lessons occur so you become more conscious of the need for compassion in your relationships. Karma is therefore a tool to teach you whatever life-lessons will most effectively help you evolve. Suffering is not necessary in life, but we must accept it when it occurs because it is designed to help us evolve. While we must be accepting of whatever trials come to us; at the same time we must learn to free ourselves from negative Karma.

Dharma is also a tool for learning and personal evolution. Assuming you did not steal, murder or lie in another lifetime, your Higher Self may still decide to experiment a bit, perhaps in order to better understand life as a human being. To facilitate that understanding, your Higher Self may create trials and events in your life, so that the desired learning can take place. There is usually less suffering in the lessons of Dharma than in the lessons of Karma; sometimes there is no suffering at all.

Even though you are seeking personal evolution, you may have suffered some trial or injustice that seems unbearable to you. When this is the case you may wish to call upon the Great Justice of the Universe to manifest itself in your life and the lives of those directly around you. We are not only talking about invoking simple human justice here, also we refer to calling on the Divine Justice that sets experiences in place so that our Karma will be resolved, in order to free the soul of its burden. If you believe you have suffered injustice at the hands of another, you can call upon the Great Justice to set things right. Then, the Great Justice will cause the occurrence of events that will definitely force your aggressor into a lesson, to help him relieve his soul of its Karmic burden.

On the outside, the "target" will probably seem to suffer, and the events will appear to lead to the correction of the situation so that you receive the justice you feel you were denied. It might even ruin his/her life. In truth, these events are set up in a way that is designed to relieve both of you of the Karma that probably binds you together, and this correction might even ruin your own life. If the (named) aggressor is in the right, and it is you that is in the wrong, then get ready to experience an unpleasant major lesson, while the smiling face of your innocent companion mocks you.

High levels of compassion and forgiveness will also transmute your Karma so it is released without you having to face those difficult experiences. Developing an attitude of loving compassion will elevate your Karma until love dissolves your Karma completely, thereby removing the necessity for unpleasant lessons from your life. Compassion can prevent painful lessons from occurring; then again it will also prevent the lesson from being received. Perhaps, in that event, the lesson was not necessary for you to evolve, and the events you are experiencing may have just been the extra weight of your past Karma, from a time when you were less virtuous than you are now.

The key here is to find a balance between accepting the lessons of life on the one hand, and forgiving and developing compassion as a tool to relieve the pain of your existence on the other hand. The practice of compassion consists of identifying the lessons in your life by getting a perspective that is external to your normal point of view; it is as if you were a Spirit flying above your human self. As you look down on the problems in your life, and the people you are having trouble dealing with, you must actively work on forgiving the other parties that you have been angry with, at the same time seeking understanding of the lesson itself, and its meaning in your life. Breathe deeply and do not be afraid of experiencing the emotions from your past. Replay your life in your mind, and ask your God to guide you through the steps of your Karmic lessons and your Dharmic path.

In time, you will learn how to call upon the Great Justice to manifest itself, without negative repercussions, but don't do this technique until you are comfortable in your heart, since it will bring up old memories and it will manifest events that may cause you to suffer, if you have not first developed enough compassion, and the ability to see your life from a higher perspective.

Lessons of the Mind

Meditation

The Green Dragon at the White Gate

This meditation is based on breathing and visualization. You will breathe deeply and softly. Sit down cross-legged on a pillow (or on a chair if you can't cross your legs). Do not rest your back on anything. Practice using your stomach muscles to hold your spine straight, without excessive effort. As you begin the deep breathing and maintain this position, you will also use the Pran Mudra (hand position), explained in the basic hand mudras section. Please become familiar with it before beginning this meditation practice. (Pran is a mudra, Prana is a form of energy.)

Visualize drawing green energy up from the earth. Breathe as you visualize that emerald green energy rising from the earth, entering your base Chakra and legs, filling your body completely with green light, all the way up to your head. Visualize the green light surrounding you, flooding you from the inside of your body and extending to the area surrounding you. Visualize this for a few minutes.

Now, empty your mind. Forget about the green light; just leave the light to do its work. Begin to visualize drawing white light down from the Heavens, entering the top of your head until it fills your entire body. Visualize this for a few minutes.

There is a place called the "door of Prana", at the bridge of your nose, between your eyes. It is just inside your nasal area, where you initially feel air flowing in when you inhale, in the area where your nose joins your eye bridge. Concentrate on the door of Prana. Breathe, and feel the air slowly going back and forth in this area of your nose. See your body filled with white light, and concentrate continuously on the door of Prana. From this place in your nose the Prana enters. This is the Universal life force, a form of energy latent in the air around you. The Prana enters your body as you inhale, but it doesn't leave your body when you exhale. Your body retains this life force and it circulates freely inside of you. When you exhale, only depleted air is evacuated. Visualize the white light shining brighter and brighter at the bridge of your nose while the white light/ Prana / life force is circulating throughout your body. Continue this technique for five minutes.

Empty your mind, relax, and be at peace.

Prana gives life

In scientific terms we recognize that Prana is actually the sub-atomic particles of energy which are freely available in the air around us. As you fill yourself with this Life Force, you will be surprised at how much energy and vitality it will bring to you. With practice, as your body learns to remain calm and relaxed while you practice, you may extend the period of breathing in the white light to ten minutes, and then to twenty minutes.

Hands of God

Basic Hand Mudras

A "mudra" is a hand gesture, just as a "mantra" is a sound and a "mandala" is an image or thought. A mudra is a particular position of your hands that connects the energy channels in your fingers in certain ways, in order to produce a precise and beneficial effect. When the tips of specific fingers touch, this action activates energy relays which, in conjunction with the normal flow of energy through your straightened fingers, produces specific desirable affects in your physical and energetic bodies.

Some mudras are designed to stimulate their beneficial effects in your physical body, while others are designed to affect your spiritual bodies. Effects of the physical mudras range from rebuilding your bones and cartilage, to healing your kidneys, to clearing your mind, to helping you to get up more quickly in the morning. spiritual mudras have a broad range of elevating effects that can enhance your psychic abilities, help you forgive, reduce anger, raise your energy level, etc. In fact, there are hundreds of different mudras. From these you may create all the effects you could possibly wish for, but it is recommended that you learn them one at a time.

Pran Mudra

This mudra stimulates the base Chakra, the channels of energies in the legs, and the minor Chakras in the middle of the feet. This mudra is called "Mudra of Life". It elevates the energy level, reduces fatigue, and clears your eyesight. It will enhance your determination and self-trust. It is also used in conjunction with treatments for eye disorders.

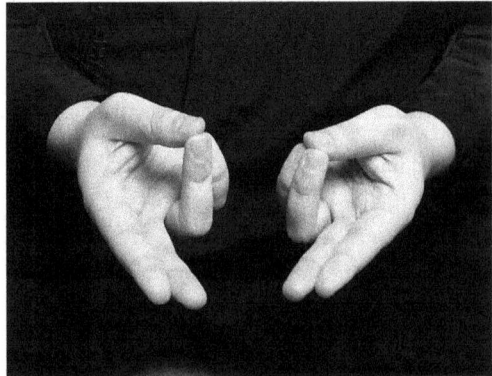

Straighten your index and middle fingers; place your thumb against your ring and your little fingers at the tips, forming a circle. Take deep, slow, Normal Breaths. Concentrate on your base Chakra and the soles of both feet. To begin: After a minute of breathing normally, begin Reversed Breathing and continue for several cycles. Breathe in and tighten your abdomen, sexual organs, perineum and buttocks. Hold your breath in for five seconds and then release everything, except the mudra. Breathe normally again and repeat this cycle for five minutes.

Knowledge Mudra

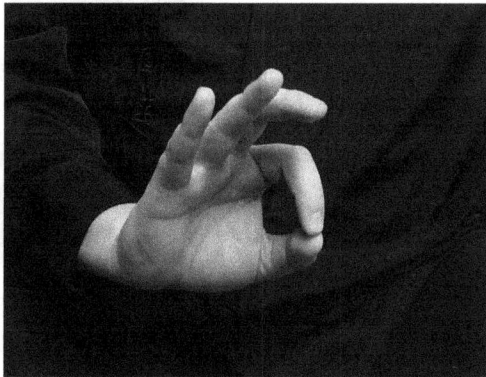

This mudra stimulates the ability to learn and teach. It is the mudra of knowledge. Using this mudra makes it easier for both sides of your brain to link new neurons together, (thus forming connections that are the basis for inspiration and the aggregation of new knowledge). These neural connections also enable you to communicate information more easily, and more effectively. The Knowledge Mudra is also useful for acquiring knowledge from the Heavens, for learning subconsciously, and for allowing your Higher Self to guide you.

You will notice that many statues of Buddhist Gods are shown using this mudra.

The Knowledge Mudra is performed with your palms pointing forward and your fingers pointing up. Touch your thumb and index fingers together at the tips, allowing them to form a gentle curve. Breathe normally, focusing on the area where your fingertips touch. Empty your mind and be at peace.

Healing Mudra

The Healing Mudra is often used by the Buddha called Sange Menla. who brought the science of healing to Buddhism. It will help your body create a supportive environment for healing, so the medical and alternative solutions you employ have a better chance of working. It is not meant to be a replacement for medical solutions, it supports those therapies. Sange Menla is also known in Sanskrit as Baishajye Guru.

The hand position for the Healing Mudra is the same as it is for the Knowledge Mudra, but your fingers must be pointing downwards. Sit with your legs crossed, with your left hand resting on the spot where your legs cross, palms up in front of your Dantian, while your right hand is placed in the shape of the mudra, with your right wrist resting on your right knee. Breathe deeply and slowly, and meditate.

Opening Gate Mudra

This mudra is often used in those ceremonies used to open the Gates of the Temple. It is the mudra that improves listening and communication. It will treat any throat disorder and this mudra also helps you develop the ability to communicate at the physical and spiritual levels.

The top photo shows how to place your hands when you do the mudra, but the lower photo shows more clearly that you wrap your left thumb inside the fingers of your right hand. Touch your right thumb and your left middle finger, and notice the sea shell shape. Breathe, relax, feel the energy flowing through your hands and your throat. Use the mantra "OM" softly to enhance the effects of this exercise.

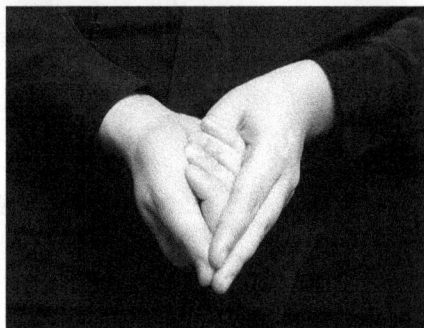

Food, Air and Energy Mudras

The Food, Air and Energy Mudras are utilized to improve the assimilation of the food and fuels you consume. When the strain of assimilating the food you eat is markedly reduced, your health will naturally be enhanced. Moreover, your energy level will soar. This mudra is designed to help you process food, absorb the nutrients from that food, and then to eliminate the waste products more efficiently. The Food, Air and Energy Mudras offer all of these benefits, and they will also help you to resolve digestive problems.

Assimilation Mudra

With the left hand, link your thumb, middle and ring fingers. This will link the circulation of energy with the assimilation/elimination process of all your bodies (physical and spiritual). With your right hand, link your thumb, index and middle finger, which will enhance the assimilation process at all levels. Breathe for two to five minutes, keeping your hands in this position. Relax and empty your mind.

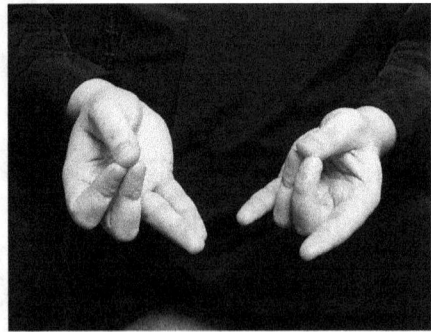

Elimination Mudra

Keep your left hand in the same position as the previous mudra, so you stay in touch with the flow of energy from the assimilation process just established.

It is only necessary to change your right hand position, linking your thumb, ring and little fingers, while keeping the index and middle finger straight. This mudra will enhance your ability to eliminate waste and toxins, help to heal digestive illnesses, and is especially beneficial for intestinal upsets. Breathe for a few minutes with your hands in this position. Concentrate on the flow of the energy, relaxing your mind and body completely.

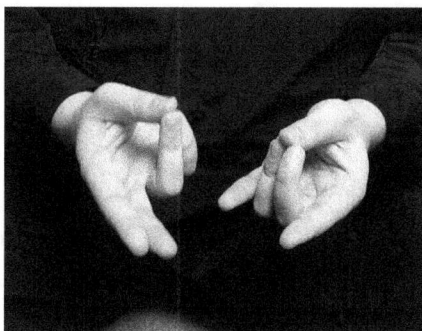

Elemental Mudras

The Elemental Mudras are a good way to tap into the elemental forces of which everything in nature is comprised. Each of the Elemental Mudras encourages your energetic body to channel the five types of primal energy: Spirit (Void), earth, air, fire and water. When you channel these elemental forces properly, you can heal yourself more effectively and you can learn to direct these forces to manifest your desires. These mudras should be used before any type of exercise that make use of the primal Elements. They may also be used alone, for the simple benefits they bring as we reconnect to the primary, elemental forces of the universe. .

Each finger of the hand is associated with a specific element.

The thumb is associated with the most abstract element, which is the Void or Spirit. The Void is not a form of emptiness; rather, it is an absolutely infinite Primal Element that cannot be defined in normal human terms. Thus, it is perceived as a Void, from our limited human perspective. Using the mudra of the Void is a good way to attain peace of mind and creativity. The Void will connect you with the spiritual world and bring its light and wisdom into your life. The Void will also help you attain the state of «no mind» for which there is no simple explanation: experience must serve as the teacher in this regard.

The index finger is associated with the Air Element. Air is swift and conveys knowledge to us in its flowing streams. The Air Element enhances mental acuity and general intelligence.

The middle finger is associated with the Fire Element. Fire is a powerful element, which has penetrating and transmuting properties. The Fire Element enhances power and courage.

The ring finger is associated with the Water Element. Water is associated with the characteristics of emotion, motion and sensibility. The Water Element also helps us to develop flexibility and good circulation.

The little finger is associated with the Earth Element. The Earth Element brings stability and strength. Its nature is to be grounded, stable, and solidly in contact. Therefore it increases these characteristics in you.

Each of these mudras naturally uses all of your fingers together. However, the overall shape of the hand in each of the mudras is used to emphasize on the element associated with that finger. These mudras also connect the energy channels (Meridians) in ways that create the desired effect. Take note that the Chakras do not necessarily correspond to the associated element in every technique, but they do in this particular application. The concepts exposed by this particular exercise should be contemplated during the practice. Form your hands into the shape of the mudra, and as you breathe, visualize the colors and focus on the related Chakra.

Chi – Earth

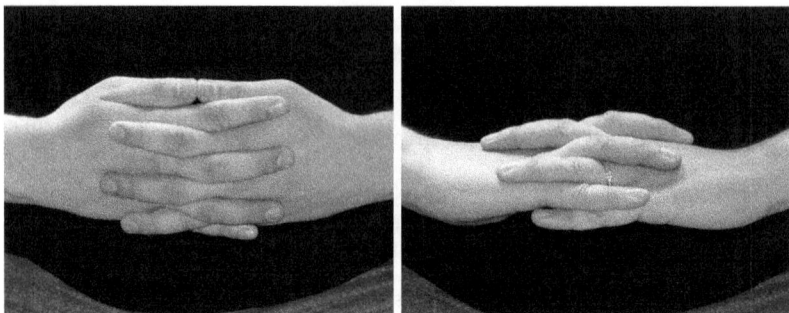

Place your hands as shown above, with your fingers intertwined and the tips of your thumbs touching. This represents the low gravitational center and stability of the Earth Element. The photo on the left represents the best way to do it, with palms facing down. The photo on the right is only to show you the proper finger position, with the thumbs touching.

As you perform this mudra, you may focus on your base Chakra, which is at the base of your spine. Feel yourself become one with all things that are solid. Feel yourself become part of the very earth beneath you. Imagine your body as an almost inflexible rock. Be aware of your physical body, its solidity and the reality of it. Visualize the colors brown and aquamarine (pale green) everywhere. Breathe a bit faster than normal. Say the mantra "Chi" a few times, aloud or mentally. Feel the emotion of enduring stability.

Sui – Water

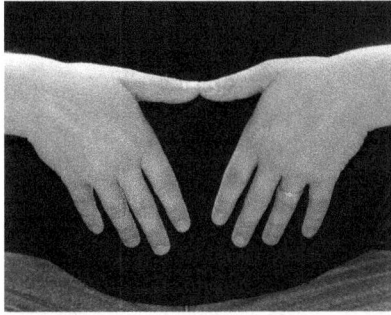

Place your hands as above, with all of your fingers hanging down in front of your belly, representing free flowing water.

Concentrate on your lower abdomen where you might feel the energy swirling and gurgling like water in your Dan-tian. Concentrate on your Navel Chakra. Begin to feel yourself flow with nature. Allow your body to move a bit. Water is the element of emotion, fluidity and flexibility. Visualize everything bathed in the color blue. Breathe normally and repeat the mantra "SUI".

Ka - Fire

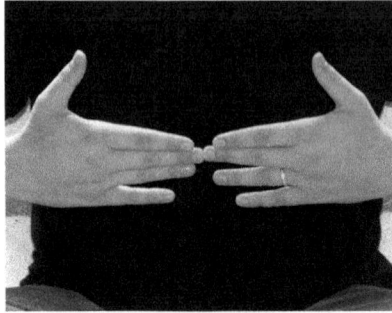

Touch the tips of your middle fingers together. The thumbs are pointing up, to represent the force of Fire rising. Start the mudra with your hands in front of your solar plexus and, after a while, lift your hands up gently until they are in front of your Heart area.

You should begin by focusing on your solar plexus, then on your Heart Chakra. You may feel your body being comfortably consumed in a rising tide of great warmth. Visualize everything around you in the color of red flames, with streams of green flowing through them. Focus on being courageous. While your hands are in front of your solar plexus, breathe a little bit faster than normal, and say the mantra "Ka". As you raise your hands in front of your Heart, slow your breathing down and feel yourself becoming more internal; softly chant the mantra (Ka).

Being courageous has nothing to do with living without fear; courage is acting without paying attention to your present fears.

When you are angry, do the Ka mudra to temper your anger and to develop more compassion. The appeasing energies of this mudra will help you to moderate your anger and ease your tensions. Hold the mudra longest in front of your Heart.

Fu - Wind

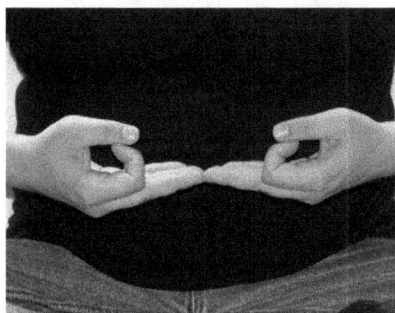

Hold your index fingers so they touch your thumbs, tip to tip, forming two small circles. The middle fingers should be touching and the rest of your fingers should also be extended. Place your hands (in mudra position) in front of you, anywhere that feels comfortable. The completed energy circuit is formed with your arms, with your throat Chakra at the top of the circuit and the mudra at the bottom of the circuit.

Focus on your throat Chakra. Feel free, subtle and untouchable. Nothing can stop you, and nothing can disable you. You should visualize everything around you radiating bright yellow energy, with purple waves and gentle clouds surrounding you. Let your mind connect to the source of all knowledge. You won't really feel any effect until a sufficient period of training has passed, but you will train your mind by contemplating these concepts. Allow peace to flood throughout your entire being. Breathe normally and say the mantra "Fu".

Ku - Void

The left palm is held face up, and the right hand is turned so that the palm is towards you. Your thumbs should be extended. You should slide your hands together, so your hands intersect, with two fingers on either side of the intersection. The photo on the left is the proper way to do the mudra, with palms facing up and towards you. The photo on the right shows the hands slightly rotated to show you how the hands intersect.

The left hand draws energy from above, and the right hand gives that energy to your body. This mudra allows these energies to intertwine in a single confluence.

Your focus here should be on your Third Eye and your Crown Chakra. Visualize yourself at the center of the Void, at its very center. See yourself in all things, and visualize everything in existence as part of you. With this thought, everything external and internal to you is one with you. Breathe as slowly as possible without straining. Say the mantra "Ku", once or several times, then empty your mind. With every inhalation, hold your breath in for a few seconds, and with every exhalation, hold it out for a few seconds.

Experiencing the Void is an essential part of the Elemental Mudra practice. The Void connects the other four elements with the Universe. Contemplate this truth: "I am everything and nothing. I am everywhere and nowhere. I am one with the universe. I AM."

Kuji Goshin Ho

Whatever the technique, it is always better to receive a sacred initiation in person from a competent Master, than to simply read a technique from a book. Nonetheless, in the absence of a competent Master, a competently written book may offer you the only resource available for you to receive any kind of initiation whatsoever. The techniques presented in this book are not the equivalent (nor can they take the place of) the kind of mastery of the all-inclusive techniques achievable after years of training with a Master; However, this book is a very good place to start if you sincerely desire to climb the staircase that leads to spiritual discovery. The process of learning these techniques can efficiently help you to start climbing that ladder within only a few weeks of daily practice, but you should never think you have found the truth until you reach actual illumination.

If you want to have the best chance at attaining the results you desire, you must develop an attitude of respect and reverence for the sacred nature of the Divine world. This reverent attitude must be your first priority when you begin to study, learn and practice the techniques of Kuji-In, the first step in learning from this book. If you want real results from your studies here, you must begin with the proper context. Arrange your environment so that it is peaceful. Make sure you will not be interrupted during your training session for any reason. (For example, unplug your phone, make sure there are no visitors, and that nothing will interrupt you in any way) You must assure yourself that your environment is inviolate. A sacred space requires quiet. You cannot achieve success when you are harried and your outer world is in chaos. This is your consecrated Holy place; that place where you connect with your own Divine Light or Self. Treat it as hallowed ground. Do not even play music in the background unless it is necessary to shut out noise from the outside world.

"Kuji Goshin Ho" is the expression we use to refer to the protective aspects of this sacred practice. Goshin = protection. Ho = ritual. The first aspect you will learn from Kuji-In is the protective virtues at many levels, which includes the enhancement of the natural regeneration of the body, and the clearing of the mind from outside influences.

In fact, these practices and techniques are the rungs of the ladder you are climbing. With each step up the ladder, you will add a level of protection to your daily life. You do not have to consciously think about achieving these increasing levels of protection, they will occur automatically as you perform the energy techniques. As your bodily energetic systems develop, many events will occur in ways you did not plan, so powerful are the influences these techniques have on your immediate environment. The Kuji-In techniques will change your life. If you practice a lot, the effect will be drastic and could cause minor, but temporary disease manifestations. Take care of yourself; you must act responsibly with your newly acquired abilities.

Warning! If you use Kuji-In to harm anyone else, even if they seem deserving to you, it will not matter what negative emotion is driving your intention, (anger, hatred, jealousy, avarice…). If you push forward in your Kuji-In practice, while harboring ANY such intentions and emotions, the result will be an extremely quick resolution of the karmic weight attached to the event in question. This means that you might turn your own life into a living hell. These are the inevitable consequences if you pray to God to punish someone, or to bring money to you without even working for it, or you pray that someone is manipulated into falling in love with you. You are totally responsible for the consequences of everything that you experiment with. You will have all the tools necessary to make your life into whatever you want it to be. There is never any need to act from negative or manipulative emotions. Therefore, in EVERY situation, act with virtue.

Practicing Kuji-In as it is presented here will support and enhance every other action you take in life. Your psychic powers will evolve, and you will achieve an expanded perception of the world. As you practice these techniques, concentrate on doing them for the joy of learning them, with no other reason than discovering your true self and elevating your consciousness. Once you have completed a period of practice, you can use various manifestation techniques in conjunction with these present techniques with a drastically enhanced efficiency.

Kuji-In Techniques

Kuji-In is translated from the Japanese as "Nine Syllables". The number nine is the number that symbolizes completion in the Buddhist system. Your hands are your primary tool in these practices, and each hand mudra is combined with a specific mantra/sound, mandala/visualization and breathing exercise that completes the technique. Thus, each set is comprised of a mudra/mantra/mandala, and will be referred to as a SET for the remainder of this text. The Kuji-In technique is composed of nine SETS.

In Kuji-In practice you will be combining these three elements ((movement (mudra)/ sound (mantra)/thought (mandala/mind)) in order to manifest your desires. (Again remember that your goal for now is to perform the daily practices for the joy of learning these techniques and for the pleasure of connecting to your Divine Self). For each SET you will make the hand signs (mudra), say the single word repeatedly (mantra), and visualize the effect of the set to the best of your knowledge (mandala/mind). Start with the first set, (the RIN Mantra), using only that one syllable mantra. Repeat this mantra in your mind, while you also position your hands according to the mudra, and focus your mind on the concept associated with the mudra/mantra. Focus without conscious effort. Let your mind simply settle down until it rests on that thought. Do not judge yourself harshly if your mind wanders in every direction; simply come back peacefully to the practice.

Do not move on to the next set until you are comfortable with the three parts of the first set: get comfortable with using your hands (mudra), together with the indicated word (mantra) and thought (mandala). When you master the three parts of a single set, and you feel that something is starting to happen in the energy planes, you can move to the next set. Each set may take as little as a day, or as much as a month of daily practice before you can feel its effect. Practice periods may vary between five minutes and an hour every day. If you don't feel anything after a few days of practice, move on to the next set. Eventually, you will feel the energies actively working on your body.

When you reach the ninth set, you will start learning more complex mantras; these are complete prayers. At this juncture it is best that you begin with the first set again and re-climb the ladder. This will greatly enhance the efficiency of your Kuji-In practices, and the Divine Forces will be more present to work with you during your practices. This form of mantra is a prayer, thus it is uttered repeatedly with faith. Say it just as you would speak any normal phrase that deserves to be spoken with reverence. It is to your True Self that you are praying.

Before you begin each practice period, start with a few minutes of the general breathing exercise. Then, for each practice period, start with the first set (RIN), and continue with each set in sequence for one full minute, followed by the next set (for one minute), one after the other, until you reach the set that you are currently learning/working on. You may practice the set you are currently working on for as long as you wish.

Once you have gone through the process of learning the entire Kuji-In system, a normal practice period can be accomplished over thirty minutes as follows: One minute of breathing, three minutes per set (total twenty-seven minutes), and two minutes of silent contemplation. You may then meditate for another half hour to elevate your consciousness.

In the following presentation, the first photo demonstrates the best way to do each exercise and the second photo shows you the proper finger placement for that exercise. The instructions for each mudra are followed by the Chakra associated with that Kuji, the mantra prayer to be spoken with it, and the concepts and benefits associated with practicing the Kuji. Take note that the word "On" (from the Japanese) is like the "Om" in Sanskrit, but the "On" involves a projection of the mantra, while the "Om" is more contemplative and internal. A "Kanji" may be also added to your visualization. A Kanji is a Japanese symbol representing one letter of a word. Next to the picture of the mudra, you will see a small square. The Kanji for this Kuji-In is the small letter at the center of the square. You may add the Kanji to your visualization.

Here is a list of the 9 Kuji-In sets with their japanese titles, associating each with their popular benefits.

1- RIN – Reinforces the positive aspects of the physical, mental and energetic planes.

2- KYO – Increases the healthy flow of energy, mastery of energy.

3- TOH – Enhances your positive relationship with the universe, resulting in improved harmony and balance.

4- SHA – Develops enhanced healing, regeneration.

5- KAI– Develops foreknowledge, premonition, intuition, feeling.

6- JIN – Increases telepathic ability, communication, knowledgeability.

7- RETSU – Enhances your perception and mastery of space-time dimensions.

8- ZAI – Fosters a relationship with the Elements of creation.

9- ZEN – Results in Enlightenment, completeness, suggestive invisibility.

Tools and application

Although the only apparent features would be the commonly seated posture holding some kind of hand position, this Nine Hand Seals method actually combines five main tools:

- a hand position, called "mudra" in sanskrit
- a spoken expression, called "mantra" in sanskrit
- a focus point in the body, called "chakra" in sanskrit
- a mental visualization, called "mandala" in sanskrit
- a philosophical concept, called "dharma" in sanskrit

All or a few of these tools are used while breathing in a relaxed posture. The beauty of this technique is that it can be done by combining only two of the five tools, helping in the assimilation of the technique, yet it reaches its full potential when all the tools are applied at once. This way, it becomes much easier to assimilate each step one by one.

When to Use

The techniques can be used from a few minutes to a full hour each day. It works great right before you go to bed. In time, the practice of the technique will automatically put you in a state of relaxation and inner awareness, most of the time at the cost of a lesser awareness of the surroundings. It is the goal to attain. You will naturally generate your own mental cocoon when you practice, thus it becomes necessary to warn you of an important side effect. If you start doing even a part of the technique while you are driving your car, or doing something that requires your attention, you might get into this isolated mental state for a moment, putting yourself and other people at risk. It is often stronger than your own will to drive carefully. Practicing this technique will put you in a state of inner awareness. You would not like to use this wonderful technique to lose your concentration when it is the most critical. So, we recommend you practice the Nine Hand Seals techniques in a suitable place for it, when your concentration is not required to keep you and other people safe.

Since this technique focuses your attention within yourself, it is not a technique to use while you are actually training or performing some other activity that requires your attention. Even if the techniques will give out great benefits by themselves, the Nine Hand Seals assists your development by making your potential fully available when you need it in your other training processes. In this sense, an athlete must not use the Nine Hand Seals or its component tools while he is doing his actual routine, but before it, or use the mental focus tools when simply training in the gym. In the same manner, a musician will only disturb his concentration if he tries to hold the mental concepts in mind while also trying to play with efficiency, but having practiced the

Nine Hands Seals before, more neural connections will be available for him to benefit from his practice.

For example, the first technique is used to develop both physical strength and self-confidence. Those who practices enough of the first technique will have quicker results when bodybuilding, and faster recovery periods between each training. A businessman who takes the time to use the full technique 15 minutes each day for a week will feel much more comfortable afterwards, when doing his presentations or holding negotiations.

Mudras

The body is filled with nerves that carry electricity, but it also has a more subtle circuitry, known as meridians. These meridians are commonly used in traditional Chinese medicine in the application of acupuncture. They are also the base of many massage techniques, since they have many beneficial influences on the body and the mind. Their use normally induces a state of relaxation, making the body prone to recovery.

The hand positions, or mudras, that we will use crosses and extends the fingers in ways to benefit from these meridians. Even though the meridians travel through the whole of the body, most of them start and end at the fingertips, thus, the hand positions and finger puzzles. When you breathe while concentrating on focus points or acupressure points, it will work on these points in the same way a needle or massage would.

In ancient India, the Hindu people tried out every type of: body positions, meditations, endless recitation of prayers, difficult fasting, applying many trials on their minds and bodies, in a quest for the ultimate yoga of self-development. One of the legacies of these experiments was the use of mudras that worked on the body and the mind in manners similar to what yoga would do. Yet, these hand positions are much simpler to apply than holding full body postures. These hand positions traveled to China and Japan along with the propagation of philosophy and meditation techniques.

Mantras

The spoken expressions we will use always represent a reference to the philosophy that we keep in mind, yet it is spoken to accelerate the effect of the technique. It is known in auto-suggestions and neural programming that even though we keep a thought in mind, the concept integrates the mental process much faster if it is spoken aloud, since it uses more parts of the brain to speak than if the concept is only mentally contemplated. The words can be spoken in any language, since the important thing is to involve the brain in physical speech. While many practitioners of Japan's kuji-in appreciate speaking the Japanese kanji pronounciation, some healers and spiritualists prefer the Sanskrit mantra, while some people also like to speak them in their common language. Here, we will give the Japanese Kanji pronounciation (jp) and the Sanskrit pronounciation (sk.) for each of the nine steps.

Nevertheless, the original mantras are in Sanskrit, coming from an ancient ritual or reverence to Indra, the concept of a divine bridge between the origin of the universe, and the practitioner. The Hindu god Indra was believed to be the God of all minor gods. It's another way to say that all the various universal forces, once called "gods", are all united under a single universal concept.

The concrete affirmations of philosophical expressions are a key component for mental training, as it reinforces the concepts they represent in our mind. While repeatedly reciting a few words that hold a certain meaning, the speech interacts with subconscious parts of our mind to make new connections and render the concept more accessible to our awareness, in our conscious mind. Although the spoken expressions used in our techniques might seem to differ a bit from the philosophical concept held in mind, their efficiency is used to its fullest since they work in combination with the mental concept. This entire aspect will become much simpler when you are finished learning the first technique.

Mandala

Visualization is an image that we imagine in our mind. Mental visualization is there to help us keep our attention on the technique, hoping to prevent the mind to wander too far astray. Yet, if you start to think about random subjects, do not put pressure on yourself to come back to the visualization, but try to come back in a peaceful and relaxed attitude, calmly resetting the imagery in your mind.

The image kept in mind will assist in placing our attention on the focus point, but it will also use colours in ways known as chromotherapy (colour therapy), combining the psychological effect of the colour to enhance the efficiency of our practice period. Of course, the visualization itself will have a subtle reference to the philosophical concept held in mind. These visualisations are suggestions, and will vary from one tradition to another. We will even give out different visualisations in future books.

Chakras

When we pay attention to a place in our body for a long enough period of time, the focus point will become relaxed and our awareness of this place will be enhanced. Paying attention to a part of our body will accelerate its healing or regeneration, since our mental attention does lend more neural electricity to the area of attention. This available extra energy is always used in the best possible way by the body. For example, people who use pain killers heal slower than those who do not, since feeling pain continually attracts our attention to the hindered area. While the time difference is not miraculous, it is notable. Each of our nine techniques requires us to focus on a specific point in the body, not to heal it but to enhance it. These focus points, specific to each of the nine techniques, are simultaneously a part of the meridians system, nervous system, and endocrine system, associated with an acupressure point, a main nervous centre and a gland.

When focusing on a point in your body, it should be done in a relaxed attitude. It is not necessary to concentrate with force. Simply pay attention to the focus point and try to feel it. It might take quite a while before you feel any particular sensation at this focus point, and it is not required. The moment you pay attention to a specific place on your body, the technique will be enhanced.

1- RIN

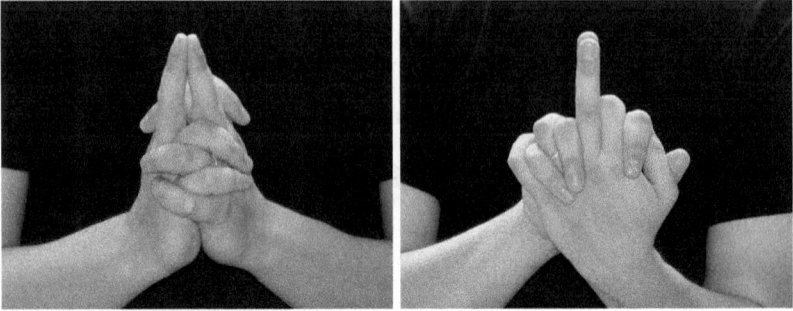

Extend your two middle fingers and interlace all other fingers.

Chakra: Base

Mantra jp: On baï shi ra man ta ya sowaka

Mantra sk: Om vajramanataya swaha

The RIN set is used to strengthen your mind and body. This Kuji-in set must be performed before any other Kuji-in sets can truly be effective. The RIN Kuji acts as a sort of hook-up to the Ultimate Source of all Power. By connecting you with this Divine energy, the RIN Kuji strengthens your mind and body, especially in collaboration with the other practices of the Kuji-In. A stronger connection to the Divine energy source will make you stronger at every level. Please be aware that this set may elevate your body temperature.

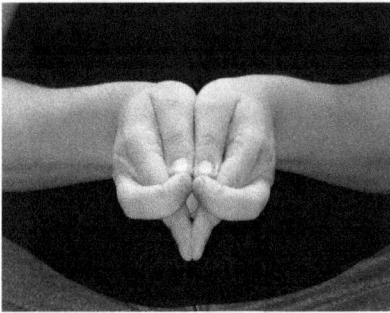

Extend your index fingers and bend your middle fingers over your index fingers so that the tip of your thumbs are touching. Interlace all your other fingers.

Chakra: Hara/Navel

Mantra jp: On isha na ya in ta ra ya sowaka

Mantra sk: Om ishaanayaa yantrayaa swaha

KYO activates the flow of energy within your body and outside of you, in your environment. This Kuji will help you learn to direct energy throughout your body, and eventually outside your body, so you can manifest your desires in the objective world. Although willpower directs energy, you must not push too hard with your willpower. Willpower that is used to direct energy should be rather like "wanting something a lot" but not like "getting a stranglehold on something, or pushing with a crippling force". Even when you apply your willpower to attain something you desire, you must always be at peace and relaxed.

3- TOH

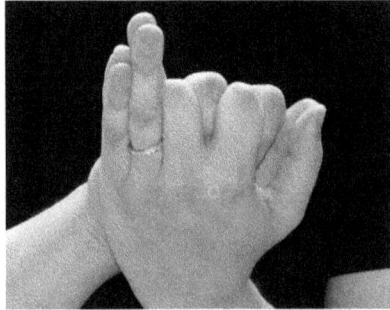

Point your thumbs and the last two fingers of both hands while keeping your index and middle fingers interlaced inside your hands.

Chakra: Dan-tian, between the Hara and the Solar Plexus

Mantra jp: On je te ra shi ita ra ji ba ra ta no-o sowaka

Mantra sk: Om jitraashi yatra jivaratna swaha

By practicing TOH, you will develop your relationship with your immediate environment, and eventually with the entire universe. As you practice, begin by filling yourself with energy and then surround yourself with this energy. (This is accomplished by visualizing that it is so). This is the Kuji of harmony. It teaches you to accept the outside events of life while remaining at peace inside. Always breathe deeply inside your abdomen, naturally, without strain.

4- SHA

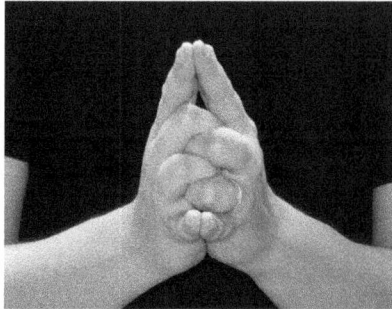

Extend your thumbs, index fingers and both little fingers. Interlace your middle and fourth finger inside your hands.

Chakra: Solar Plexus

Mantra jp: On ha ya baï shi ra man ta ya sowaka

Mantra sk: Om haya vajramaantayaa swaha

With this Kuji, the healing ability of your body is increased. As you practice this set, your body will become more efficient in its daily rebuilding, healing and reconstruction. This increased healing efficiency is the result of the higher levels of energy passing through your energy channels (Meridians) and your solar plexus. This healing vibration will eventually radiate around you, causing other people to heal as you spend time with them.

5- KAI

Interlace all of your fingers, with the tip of each finger pressing into the root of the facing finger.

Chakra: Heart

Mantra jp: On no-o ma ku san man da ba sa ra dan kan

Mantra sk: Om namah samanta vajranam ham

This Kuji will raise your awareness and help you to develop your intuition. The mudra is called "The outer bonds". The outer bonds are the energy currents that precede every event, if only for an instant. They are the specific influence from the outside world that produces every one of your experiences.

Intuition is a powerful ally; it is the way you perceive what your senses register from your contact with the environment, and from the people surrounding you. This set will increase your intuition and will help you to learn to love yourself and others.

6- JIN

Interlace all your fingers, with your fingertips inside, each of them touching the equivalent tip of the other hand's finger, if possible.

Chakra: Throat

Mantra jp: On aga na ya in ma ya sowaka

Mantra sk: Om agnayaa yanmayaa swaha

The "inner bonds" are the energy currents inside you that connect you with your True Self. We have the ability to know what others are thinking. By reaching deep inside you, into the place with no words, you may get in contact with this same place in others. When you make this connection you may hear the other person's thoughts without words, or you may learn to communicate by thought concepts; this is commonly called telepathy.

This mudra is used to open your mind to the thoughts that others project from their mental activity. It can help you gain an understanding of why people do the things they do. If you want to develop compassion you can use this mudra to enhance your empathy for others. If you don't judge what you perceive, you will perceive it with more clarity.

7- RETSU

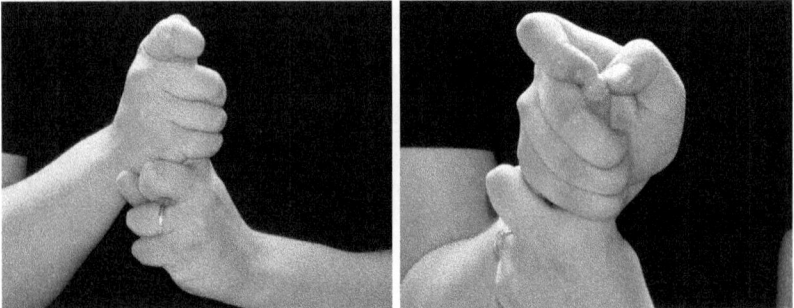

Point your left index finger up. Wrap the fingers of your right hand around your left index finger. Place the tips of your right thumb and index finger in contact with the tip of your left index finger. The fingers of your left hand are gathered into a fist.

Chakra: Jade Gate, at the back of the head
Mantra jp: On hi ro ta ki sha no ga ji ba tai sowaka
Mantra sk: Om jyotihi chandoga jiva tay swaha

After practicing the Kuji-In exercises for some time, they will alter your perception of gross matter so you will be able to perceive the different flows of energy composing our space-time multi-dimensional universe. Per the theory of relativity, as mass accelerates, time slows, thus if your energy is flowing, and you apply your willpower, your mass accelerates, time slows for you and you can simply change (or direct) the flow/ or motion of your body through space.

Now, put all this theory aside for a moment and let your mind adapt to this new perception of the Universe. Imagine that the atoms of the universe are composed of energy waves instead of rigid, inflexible solid matter; feel the flexibility of the structure of these energy waves. Understand that these energy waves build your body. You are being continuously re-created!

8- ZAI

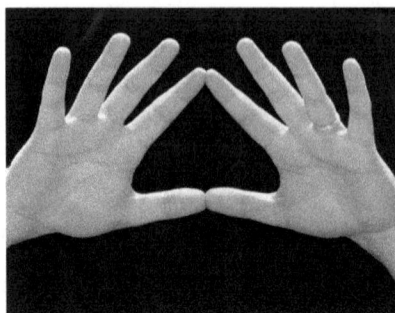

Touch the tips of your thumbs and index fingers to form a triangle, while your other fingers are spread out.

Chakra: Third Eye

Mantra jp: On Chi ri Chi i ba ro ta ya sowaka

Mantra sk: Om srija iva rtaya swaha

sRija : sh-ree-j with an almost mute "ee" after the R

Rtaya: Rutaya with an almost mute "u" after the R

By practicing with this set, you will establish a relationship with the Universal components of creation: the elements. These elements are not only physical, they are also spiritual. This Kuji practice is a basis for the power of manifestation. Visualize being in harmony with nature. Visualize the flow of Qi from nature to you, and from you to nature. After a while, notice your increasing awareness that nature is alive, and that you can communicate with it. Nature will interact with you within the limits of natural law. Eventually, as you improve your sensitivity to nature, you might develop the ability to call forth an elemental manifestation, when mastered.

9- ZEN

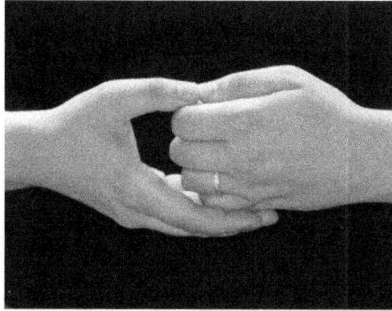

Rest your left knuckles on the fingers of your right hand, with your right palm open. Touch the tips of your two thumbs gently.

Chakra: Crown

Mantra jp: On a ra ba sha no-o sowaka

Mantra sk: Om ah ra pa cha na dhi

Illumination is the highest state of mind. Illumination is a kind of Completeness, accomplished by Meditation. By using this practice, you can eventually disappear from the common mind. You are still there, of course, but others in the common mind cannot register your presence, because your vibration is higher than what their minds can recognize or interpret as real. To practice, imagine simple emptiness, calm white light everywhere;

Then visualize melding with the white light. It is believed that to the average person you might become invisible.

Many hours of practice are required to elevate your vibration level enough to manifest the side-effects, like suggestive invisibility.

Notes on making progress:

To make progress with kuji-in, it is a good idea to have a meditation period after every complete practice period. When you "come back" from your meditation, smile and drink a glass of water. Do not neglect the smile, whether you feel like it or not. Breathe deeply and relax.

Kuji-In Additional Information

Each Kuji is dependent on the Kuji before it. For example, before you practice the fourth Kuji to enhance your healing abilities, you must do the third Kuji to produce harmony and circulation in your intestines and bowels. Before you practice the third Kuji, you must perform the second Kuji, in order to let energy circulate throughout your body. The second Kuji will open the energetic doors between your neural system and your energetic system on the ethereal plane. Before you practice the second Kuji, you must do the first Kuji to get the raw power to work with, from your base Chakra. This is why all the Kuji practices must be done in the proper order, one after the other. It is also the main reason that trying to advance too quickly in your practices will not produce as much results. If you imagine a long succession of plumbing pipes in series, leading finally to a pond, you can understand that, if you want the water to flow all the way to the pond, the valves must be open at every joint. Any restriction, (any valve that isn't open) will restrain the flow of water from reaching the next section; ultimately, if the valves aren't opened in the proper order, your pond will remain empty. The same thing is true of the flow of the Zen. The Zen energy is the water in this analogy. You must open each valve (with the correct practice) in the proper succession so that the Zen energy flows to the ultimate destination.

This list will give you an idea of the proper and necessary step-by-step process to attain a successful kuji-in experience :

1- RIN accesses power, energy, and awakens your flame.

2- KYO circulates the energy in your body, allowing it to flow in and out.

3- TOH gathers energy in your battery (bowels) and circulates it.

4- SHA distributes the energy into the necessary parts of your body, producing healing.

5- KAI allows you to Feel Everything.

6- JIN allows you to Know Everything.

7- RESTU allows you to Be Aware of Everything.

8- ZAI is a process where you become aware that everything is energy manifested.

9- ZEN connects you with the I AM.

The following visualizations are helpful variations of the Kuji-In that will make it easier for you to understand more about the functions and manifestations you will become capable of after working with these practices. Perform the complete Kuji-In practice, repeating the full prayer as a mantra, gently focusing on the corresponding Chakra, while keeping the goal of the Kuji held in your attention, then add the following visualization to your practice. It might seem demanding at first, but please try to simultaneously keep in mind as many aspects of the exercise as possible.

Complete Kuji-In Ritual Practices

First Kuji (RIN): Visualize a red shining light descending from Heaven into your body, and lighting a flame at your Base Chakra, the region between your anus and your sexual organs. Relax and begin the visualization, perform the mudra, chant the prayer mantra calmly, slowly or quickly, as you wish, (or even at an

accelerating tempo, then come back suddenly to a slower tempo. The Base Chakra is the point where the Sacred flame emerges into your energetic body.

Second Kuji (KYO): Pay attention to your Navel Chakra. Visualize your body filling with red light and the red light circulating throughout your entire body and around it. Continue paying attention to your Navel Chakra, never forcing the concentration, but always gently being aware of it.

Third Kuji (TOH): Pay attention to your Dan-tian, and visualize your entire bowel region filling with orange and golden light, which is flowing harmoniously throughout your entire bowel system healing your body. The TOH Kuji affects the harmony between you and others in your life; it enhances peace in your relationships, the joy of associations and communications, and the harmony available at the emotional level. Do this Kuji to enhance your relationships with others, as well as to heal your bowels.

Fourth Kuji (SHA): Pay attention to your Solar Plexus. Visualize it filling with a golden yellow light, pulsating with strength and peace. This is the Kuji of healing. It triggers the regeneration of your body, and the healing of every physical aspect of your health.

Fifth Kuji (KAI): Focus on your Heart Chakra while you imagine a comfortable blue light everywhere; Your heart is glowing with an intensely calm electric blue, which is so clear and strong that it radiates beyond your body. You are protected, you have intuition.

Sixth Kuji (JIN): Concentrate on your Throat Chakra, surrounding that area with blue light. Visualize a calm blue light emanating from your throat. Imagine that your body is very big, immense, much more imposing than your actual physical body. See yourself as gigantically tall, filled with the blue light which entirely envelopes you. Remain in this visualization and simply contemplate that you have access to all the knowledge of the Universe. Perceive the bonds between you and the rest of the cosmic reality: bonds of knowledge and awareness.

Seventh Kuji (RETSU): Pay attention to the area at the back of your head, at the base of your skull. You now become aware that time has no substance, matter has no substance, all is energy, and EVERYTHING is timeless eternity. Find your own simple and abstract visualization.

Eighth Kuji (ZAI): Focus on your Third Eye as you visualize yourself bathed in violet light. Know that you are the Master of your personal Universe, and that you are completely aware of your immediate Universe.

Ninth Kuji (ZEN): Your awareness shifts to and becomes one with the I AM. You contemplate the truth that: "I am. I am everything. I am everywhere. I am the Void". Clear your mind totally and allow yourself to dissolve into the complete, absolute "void" of the Spirit. God is beyond human understanding and perception. Let yourself dissolve into God; empty your mind.

Always meditate for a few minutes after you do a period of Kuji-In techniques. You must rest your mind. Breathe deeply and relax. Your energetic system will also need to rest. Stay calm, quiet and relaxed for a while after each session.

Kuji-In is a prayer, not a do-it-yourself-kit to attain power. Seek Love and Compassion; the power will come by itself. Make a place in your heart for your Spirit to play and attain joy. Make room in your mind for your Spirit to think and attain peace. The same applies to your body, since it is your Inner Temple, that place where God resides in you. Your Inner Temple is also the main site where the manifestations resulting from your practice will take place.

RIN

It may be hard for you to believe, but the Universal Fire is situated at the base of your own experience: the base Chakra at the tip of your spine. You are all that there is; you simply don't clearly understand what that means yet. On this path you will learn that, as the Sacred Flame grows brighter in you, it actually rises up your spine until it fills your entire body.

Breathe deeply and softly. Every inhalation nourishes the flame at your Base Chakra, encouraging it to fill you with Sacred Fire. Visualize the flame increasing in intensity, giving life to your entire body. As you are increasingly filled with this Sacred Fire, all the energy circuitry in your body will repair itself, becoming healthier and more alive as it receives the flow of the Universal Root energy: The Sacred Fire. This is your connection to All That IS.

Each time you make a decision, you will notice that some of your muscles tighten with fear. Muscles tighten when you have to make a decision because of the inherent biological fear that the human animal body holds. The objective of this exercise is to become conscious of the fearful nature of the human, animal part of you. Once you are aware of these fears, release them and trust yourself. Self-trust is the key to success in everything.

KYO

What you project towards others, will eventually come back to you (for good or ill) in full measure. This teaches us to keep a constant attitude of peace. Smile. Be joyful in your communications and in your actions. You will develop peace and joy as you accept it in yourself. You will discover that your experience of your environment will eventually be modified, slowly but surely by the healthy energy you nurture and project outwards. The Flame of Life will destroy your old behaviors as you establish new, healthier ways of acting and being. The ropes of energy that keep you in bondage to those old behaviors will come untied and every bond that keeps you hostage will inevitably be consumed by the Flame of Life .

As you develop this brand new, amplified, energy management system, you will discover that it is essential to become completely responsible for yourself. All that you do, all that you say, will find a way to manifest around you. You will have to learn tolerance and happiness or you will magnify your negative thoughts and these will become manifest as your reality. It is absolutely necessary to stay positive, even in the worst situations. It will be necessary to learn to feel the normal everyday emotional pains and discomforts while remaining positive; to experience those periods of depression we all have and just humbly accept them, without judgment. Keep the eyes of your Heart fixed on the higher plane of life. In fact, you will increasingly experience your growing ability to positively impact the world around you, and to manifest your desires, by nurturing healthy energy and projecting it into your environment.

TOH

Kuji-In must always be performed with an attitude of gratitude towards the infinite Universe. You must complete each action with respect. The success of your personal rituals depend on your ability to remain humble before the All, the Great spiritual Reality. When you encounter a huge obstacle, like a rock obstructing your path, instead of spending all of your energies trying to remove the rock, simply go around it. This way, even if the rock still thinks it has the power to block your path, you will be back on the road, moving ahead, keeping all your energy for some more useful purpose. Be humble on your path. You have nothing to prove to anyone, not even to yourself. Trust yourself, always.

Seek harmony with the Universe around you. When something occurs that upsets you or thwarts your plans, choose an attitude of compassion. Do not waste your energy engaging an obstacle in battle. With a strong mind, heart and body, you may advance on the evolutionary path with confidence. Even your muscles will benefit from this positive mental attitude on the path. The moment you set your mind on something, the Universal energy will always be there to assist you.

SHA

SHA teaches us that unwavering strength is always consistently available for you. That energy constantly flows into you, igniting your Sacred Flame, causing it to rise until it reaches your Solar Plexus, (the energy dispatcher). There is great power in the Universe, and it is power you can tap into at every moment. Know that you are powerful. Know also that, to manifest this power in your life, you must be ready to assume the responsibility for all your actions.

The most obvious manifestation of your new ability to circulate powerful energy, will be the complete healing of your body. Qi and Prana move in your body like rivers of fire and pure light. There are also other manifestations of this inner resource of power. Great explosions of energy may occur when you really need them. Remember that you have an equal ability to hurt and heal. This is an awesome power. You must be responsible for your actions. There are severe consequences for any misuse of this power. In this, the original intention does not matter, only the result.

KAI

As you use KAI you will find that this new energy is now circulating with ease; the flow of energy grows and begins to expand beyond the illusionary boundaries of your body. It is time to listen, time to tune in to your inner ear. You will perceive this outer world through your inner self only if you are available to receive the information. If you are convinced that you already know the truth of existence or that you have nothing to learn from others, you may be building a fence that will eventually prevent you from seeing what is on the other side. If a fence already exists, allow the fire of your Spirit to burn it to the ground. Intuition will be your most powerful guide in this process. It will reveal to you the real truth about the world that surrounds you, if you stay sensitive and available to that information.

When you practice KAI you are linked to nature and to the laws that govern the entire Universe. You are not only in contact with them, you are linked with every living thing, like the threads of a tapestry that has been woven together by the Creator of ALL. You are an active part of the living fabric of the world. If you remain attentive to your immediate surroundings you will be able to
practice, on a smaller scale, your ability to be in contact with the larger Universe. There is only one way to efficiently expand your energetic body beyond your physical boundaries; that way is to express compassion and love in every circumstance.

JIN

When you practice the JIN Kuji, you will be able to meet your Higher Self and make contact with the elevated thoughts of that more advanced part of you. There is a special part of your thinking process, hidden deep inside of you, that does not utilize words to communicate. In fact it does not speak in any language that your conscious mind understands. This place of "no words" is the place where you truly communicate, truly think and truly know. This is the place where the Divine is connected to and thinks through the human mind. Find the place with no words, and you will find this Greater Truth.

If you want to send or receive thoughts with your mind, you must understand that the thoughts that travel are not the thoughts that are phrased in words; the thoughts that travel do not depend on any form of language or system of communication. To listen without words is to accept your own inability to really understand this truth, and to learn to rely solely on your Spirit. Once you find yourself, deep inside, you will become aware of everything that comes within your mind's grasp. Only then can you decide whether or not you really want to put these concepts back into words so you can understand the thoughts and images that are flying around in the world outside of you.

RETSU

The Kuji-In RESTSU will help you to become aware that the Universe is composed of more than three spatial dimensions. According to modern quantum physics there are nine spatial dimensions and one time dimension, for a total of ten space-time dimensions. To increase your understanding of this greater reality, you must stop believing only what your senses teach you and start listening to and looking beyond the normal space-time continuum you are used to accepting as reality. The mysteries of creation will not remain secret forever if you take these steps. Naturally, your senses are necessary in your daily human experience, but when you start to acknowledge the existence of higher levels of perception, you expand your ability to see/perceive these other dimensions. Meditate to find this place of higher perception. Seek the state of transcendence, then the state of conscious transcendence.

Space-time is where you seem to exist. In fact, it is actually the place where your Higher Self is experimenting with the experience of life. The dimensions are partitions delimiting the various worlds of manifestation, but your Spirit can easily cross those boundaries, once you understand how. Develop your self-trust and faith. Believe you can do it. Be intelligent enough to notice your limits so you do not hurt yourself, but be courageous enough to go beyond those limits when you feel able to. Make peace with your physical limitations, and know that they are not meant to define your existence, only your immediate experience.

ZAI

The Elemental world is far more than the physical manifestation of Fire, Wind, Water and Earth. At the core of creation, at the moment of the birth of the Universe, at the highest level of vibration of our Universe, God chose to manifest in many forms. Each and every Element of Creation is an aspect of the

Consciousness of God.   The Elements can be classified as either the Four Elements used in Western Esotericism or the Five Elements commonly used in the Oriental Esoteric System. These systems of classification are there to aid human understanding. The basis of the ability to manifest and create is the knowledge that the Elements of Creation are absolute spiritual truths in action. They are to be praised as the origin of Creation and to be admired in their physical manifestation. By developing an attitude of consistent praise, you can form a relationship with the Elements of Creation.

Human beings are always afraid of the unknown. The most disturbing fears we suffer are the fears of the indefinite, the mysterious, the strange and occult: anything we are uncertain of makes us edgy. As we gain knowledge, we get a feeling of control that encourages us to extend a little (very fragile) trust, but even the most innocent unknown truth is always more difficult for the human mind to consider than the biggest, but most well known falsehood. With faith as your guide, you will not know fear. The unknown will stop being a dark forest filled with monsters, and become a place for you to experience the greatest adventures, and the brightest truths. When you conquer your fear of the unknown, you will find that it is the hidden doorway to God.

ZEN

ZEN teaches you to surrender yourself absolutely to the Universe. It counsels you to let go of everything you have learned: every belief, and every thought. Your human ego was a necessary tool that allowed you to learn certain lessons. Now it is time to release that ego, and to remember your smallness compared with the vast Void that is a creation of the mind of God. Standing tall, looking towards the infinite Universe, you are an infinitesimal speck, almost nothing. Put your ego in its place, and allow God to enter your life. Accept everything: every manifestation, every person, every event, and every creation, as a part of God. God can neither be grasped nor understood. God can only be Loved. When you are completely immersed in the Love of God, you will rejoin with your Divine Self, with your part of the God who made everything. Then, as you calmly contemplate the Infinite Universe, you will recognize yourself.

Conclusion: No mind

The objective of any meditative practice is to allow your mind to play with your Spirit, your True Self. The more complete the meditative method, the more physical effects will become apparent to you, and the more quickly your conscious mind will connect with your Divine Self. When you first connect with your Higher Self, you may be overwhelmed with higher thoughts. Eventually, your human mind may wish to shut down to make room for these higher thoughts; your mind will seek 'peace of mind'. Thus, When you allow your mind to be filled, it may be happy at first, until it gets inundated. At that point, simply allow your mind to shut down and look towards the Divine. As you seek these higher thoughts and permit them to fill you, you will find peace.

When you combine all of your preferred practices with the normal activities of your daily life, you make room in your mind for your Spirit. By using these profound meditations on a regular basis you will find yourselves maintaining a slightly meditative state during your other daily occupations. In time, your mind will learn to contemplate Spirit, without engaging any cognitive thinking process. This is the place of "no mind".

Never underestimate the power of Joy. Many meditative approaches deny the right of the mind to play. These approaches want to remove the human mind as soon as possible from the meditative process, pushing it out of your contemplation of God with force. This will only upset and even damage your mind. All the words, the thoughts, the methods, and the different techniques we have studied here... all these exercises allow your mind the freedom to play; when it plays, your mind is happy. Do not remove the toys of the mind too quickly. Let your mind play for as long as it wishes to. When satisfied, like a well fed baby, it will want to rest all by itself. Then your mind will be ready to peacefully contemplate the thought process of your True Self, with no words, no methods, no techniques, and especially, with no mind.

The path of enlightenment is not an objective to reach, but a process you must experience. If there is any part of the path that you overlook, your human mind misses the flavor of that spice, causing you to go through the path again until you have all the ingredients that make up the tasteful experience of life. It is not necessary for you to run through all the glens and shadows of the light and dark forests that run along each side of the path; However, the path itself must be completely traveled.

The path to Illumination lies at the foothills of the experience of Joy. Great Joy is awaiting you at every corner, even when you seem to perceive pain. With devotion to yourself, tolerance, and compassion, you will attain Joy, Love, and, in the end, Enlightenment.

In devotion to the evolution of my fellow humans, I respectfully give you this knowledge in the hope that you will reach the level of realization you seek. With Love and Compassion, I pray for the Divine to reveal itself to you, the true practitioners of the most Sacred arts.

May you be blessed,

Maha Vajra

www.ingramcontent.com/pod-product-compliance
Lightning Source LLC
Chambersburg PA
CBHW060054100426
42742CB00014B/2829